# GROUND
## UP!

# GROUND UP!

## THE ULTIMATE GROUND BEEF RECIPES & MORE!

LOVE FOOD™

This edition published by Parragon Books Ltd in 2014 and distributed by

Parragon Inc.
440 Park Avenue South, 13th Floor
New York, NY 10016
www.parragon.com/lovefood

LOVE FOOD is an imprint of Parragon Books Ltd

ISBN: 978-1-4723-2987-5

Printed in China

New recipes written by Beverly Le Blanc
Introduction and incidental text by Anne Sheasby
New internal photography by Clive Streeter
New internal home economy by Theresa Goldfinch
New cover photography by Mike Cooper
Additional design work by Geoff Borin and Siân Williams
Internal illustrations by Nicola O'Byrne and Julie Ingham

**Notes for the Reader**
This book uses standard kitchen measuring spoons and cups. All spoon and cup measurements are level unless
otherwise indicated. Unless otherwise stated, milk is assumed to be whole, eggs are large, individual vegetables
are medium, and pepper is freshly ground black pepper. Unless otherwise stated, all root vegetables should be
peeled prior to using.

Garnishes, decorations, and serving suggestions are all optional and not necessarily included in the recipe
ingredients or method. The times given are only an approximate guide. Preparation times differ according to the
techniques used by different people, and the cooking times may also vary from those given. Optional ingredients,
variations, or serving suggestions have not been included in the time calculations.

# CONTENTS

# BREAKING GROUND

Ground meat is suitable for making a wide range of delicious recipes from all over the world, many of which are hearty and homey, some of which are thrifty or frugal, but all of which are full of flavor.

Ground meat is ideal for creating tasty dishes that are economical, too. Versions of ground meat include beef, pork, lamb, turkey, chicken, venison, and veal.

Ground meat is made from various parts of the animal, usually the cheaper cuts, and it is inexpensive, but it can vary greatly in quality and fat content and this will be partly reflected in the price. Ground beef from a butcher, for example, may contain trimmings from more expensive cuts of beef. Fresh ground meat is widely available from outlets such as supermarkets, butchers, and farm shops, and many butchers will grind meat fresh to your order, if required. Some types of ground meat can also be bought frozen.

Ground red meat is a good source of protein, and the fat and saturated fat contents vary. Regular ground beef is the least expensive but fattiest choice; ground chuck is moderately priced with a good amount of fat, making it a good choice for burgers; and ground round and ground sirloin beef, the most expensive types, are less fatty and good for sauces and meatloaves.

Ground chicken is obtainable but is not so easy to find, whereas ground turkey is readily available as ground turkey or lean ground turkey breast. Ground turkey and chicken are low in fat, are a good source of protein, and can provide a lighter, healthier alternative to ground beef when made into dishes such as burgers and meatballs.

Ground pork and lamb are also available and can be used in a wide variety of recipes. Other ground meats, such as venison and veal, may not be so widely obtainable, but some supermarkets and other outlets, including butchers and online suppliers, now stock these more readily, too.

A textured vegetable protein is also available online and health-food stores as a ground meat substitute. It is a meat-free form of high-quality protein suitable for vegetarians (but not vegans, because it contains egg). It is low in fat and sodium and contains no cholesterol. It is a good source of dietary fiber. Use this vegetarian alternative to ground meat to create many ground meat recipes, including chili, burgers, and lasagna.

# COMFORTING EATS

# CREAMY CHICKEN HASH

**SERVES: 4–6**      **PREP TIME: 10 MINS**      **COOK TIME: 15–20 MINS**

## INGREDIENTS

3 tablespoons sunflower oil

1 pound fresh ground chicken

1 teaspoon dried thyme or dried dill

pinch of cayenne pepper

1 onion, finely chopped

1 large red bell pepper, seeded and finely chopped

2 large garlic cloves, finely chopped

2 tablespoons all-purpose flour

1¼ cups milk

⅔ cup frozen peas

1⅓ cups drained and rinsed canned corn kernels

salt and pepper, to taste

chopped fresh parsley, to garnish

**1.** Heat 2 tablespoons of the oil in a large skillet. Add the chicken, thyme, and cayenne pepper, season with salt and pepper, and sauté, stirring with a wooden spoon to break up the chicken into large clumps, for 4–6 minutes, until just starting to brown. Transfer to a bowl, using a slotted spoon, and set aside.

**2.** Add the remaining oil to the skillet, then add the onion and red bell pepper and sauté, stirring, for 3–5 minutes, until the onion is soft. Add the garlic and stir for an additional 30 seconds.

**3.** Sprinkle with the flour and stir for about 1 minute. Slowly stir in the milk and continue stirring until a smooth, creamy sauce forms.

**4.** Return the chicken to the skillet and add the peas and corn. Bring to a boil, stirring, then reduce the heat and simmer, uncovered, for 5 minutes, or until the peas are tender. Adjust the salt and pepper, if necessary. Garnish with parsley and serve immediately.

# CHICKEN-STUFFED SQUASH

SERVES: 4   PREP TIME: 20 MINS   COOK TIME: 1 HR

## INGREDIENTS

3 tablespoons garlic-flavored olive oil or plain olive oil

2 small or 1 large butternut squash, halved lengthwise, seeded, all the fibers removed, and the flesh slashed in a crisscross pattern

1 pound fresh ground chicken

1 red onion, finely chopped

½ teaspoon crushed red pepper flakes, or to taste

3½ cups baby spinach leaves

freshly grated nutmeg, to taste

¼ cup toasted pine nuts

⅔ cup drained and crumbled feta cheese

2 tablespoons chopped fresh parsley

salt and pepper, to taste

salad greens, to serve

**1.** Preheat the oven to 400°F. Rub 1 tablespoon of the oil over the squash halves, place them on a baking sheet, cut-side up, and roast in the preheated oven for 45 minutes, or until tender.

**2.** Meanwhile, heat the remaining oil in a saucepan over medium–high heat. Add the chicken, onion, and red pepper flakes, season with salt and pepper, and sauté, stirring with a wooden spoon to break up the chicken into large clumps, for 4–6 minutes, until cooked through.

**3.** Add the spinach and nutmeg, increase the heat, and stir until the liquid from the spinach evaporates. Transfer to a bowl and set aside.

**4.** Remove the squash from the oven (do not turn off the oven) and let stand until cool enough to handle.

**5.** Scoop out the squash flesh, retaining a thin shell. Finely chop the flesh and add to the bowl with the remaining ingredients. Toss together and adjust the seasoning, if necessary.

**6.** Divide the stuffing between the hollowed-out squash halves. Return to the oven for 10 minutes, or until the cheese is melted. If using a large squash, cut into quarters for serving. Serve with salad greens.

# BACON-WRAPPED CHICKEN BURGERS

**MAKES: 4**

**PREP TIME: 10 MINS PLUS CHILLING**

**COOK TIME: 10–15 MINS**

## INGREDIENTS

1 pound fresh ground chicken

1 onion, grated

2 garlic cloves, crushed

⅓ cup pine nuts, toasted

½ cup shredded Gruyère cheese or Swiss cheese

2 tablespoons snipped fresh chives

2 tablespoons whole-wheat flour

8 lean bacon strips

1–2 tablespoons sunflower oil

salt and pepper, to taste

## TO SERVE

4 hamburger buns, halved

red onion slices

lettuce

¼ cup mayonnaise

scallions, chopped

**1.** Put the ground chicken, onion, garlic, pine nuts, Gruyère cheese, and chives in a food processor or blender and season with salt and pepper. Using the pulse button, blend the mixture together with short sharp bursts. Scrape out onto a board and shape into four evenly sized patties. Coat in the flour, then cover and chill in the refrigerator for 1 hour.

**2.** Wrap each patty with two bacon strips, securing in place with a wooden toothpick.

**3.** Heat a heavy skillet over medium heat and add the oil. When hot, add the patties and cook over medium heat for 5–6 minutes on each side, or until cooked through and the juices run clear.

**4.** Serve the burgers in the hamburger buns with the red onion, lettuce, a spoonful of mayonnaise, and scallions. Serve immediately.

**HERO TIPS**

You can alter the flavor and texture of these luscious burgers by replacing the pine nuts with slivered almonds or unsalted cashews. If using whole nuts, first chop them, and if desired, toast lightly.

# TURKEY POT PIE

**SERVES: 4**  **PREP TIME: 20 MINS**  **COOK TIME: APPROX. 1 HR**

## INGREDIENTS

1 cup coarsely chopped green beans

1 large carrot, diced

2 bay leaves

2 tablespoons sunflower oil

1 pound fresh ground turkey

1 leek, thinly sliced

2 cups sliced chestnut mushrooms,

4 scallions, finely chopped

1 teaspoon dried tarragon

3 tablespoons all-purpose flour

⅓ cup milk

1 medium egg, beaten

1 sheet ready-to-bake rolled dough pie crust, thawed if frozen

sesame seeds, for sprinkling

salt and pepper, to taste

**1.** Preheat the oven to 375°F. Bring a large saucepan of lightly salted water to a boil, add the beans, carrot, and bay leaves and blanch for 3 minutes, or until tender-crisp. Strain, reserving ⅓ cup of the cooking liquid and discarding the bay leaves.

**2.** Meanwhile, heat the oil in a skillet. Add the turkey and leek and sauté, stirring with a wooden spoon to break up the meat into large clumps, for 3 minutes, or until it loses its raw appearance. Add the mushrooms, season with salt and pepper, and stir until the mushrooms absorb the liquid they release. Stir in the scallions, tarragon, carrot, and beans.

**3.** Sprinkle with the flour and stir for 1 minute. Stir in the milk and reserved cooking liquid and bring to a boil. Reduce the heat and simmer for 2 minutes. Adjust the seasoning.

**4.** Spoon the mixture into a 1-quart pie dish and brush the rim with egg. Add the dough, press around the edges to seal, then trim. Brush the top with beaten egg, sprinkle with sesame seeds, and cut a hole in the center. Place on a baking sheet and bake in the preheated oven for 40 minutes, or until golden brown. Serve immediately.

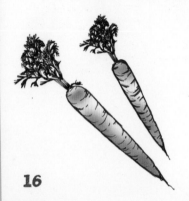

# DAILY GRIND

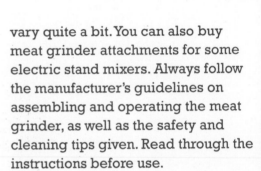

Ground meat is simply meat that has been finely chopped or broken down into smaller pieces by passing it through a meat grinder. The term "minced meat" is occasionally used for meat (such as steak) that has been finely chopped using a sharp knife.

You can buy different types of ground meat, but you can also grind or mince your own meat at home if you have some basic equipment. Grinding your own meat allows you to know the provenance of your meat and to control the quality, freshness, choice, and type of cuts going into your ground meat.

If you plan to grind your own meat on a regular basis, it's worth investing in a good-quality meat grinder. A meat grinder is a kitchen appliance that finely chops raw meat or poultry. Meat grinders vary, but the basic principle and mechanism used to grind the meat is similar. There are several types of meat grinders available, from the classic cast-iron, hand-cranked manual grinder, to the more sophisticated stand-alone, electric meat grinders, and prices vary quite a bit. You can also buy meat grinder attachments for some electric stand mixers. Always follow the manufacturer's guidelines on assembling and operating the meat grinder, as well as the safety and cleaning tips given. Read through the instructions before use.

You can also "mince," or finely chop meat using a food processor fitted with a metal blade, but you need to be careful not to overprocess the meat into mush (using the pulse button in short bursts is the best way to do this), and be sure to process the diced meat in small batches.

If you are grinding meat at home, you can choose any boneless cut of meat, depending on the recipe you are preparing it for. Try experimenting with different cuts of meat. It's good to use cuts that have some visible fat;

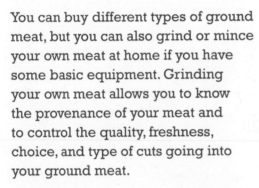

otherwise if you use meat that is very lean it will probably dry out and not be as flavorful, but be sure to trim off any tough connective tissue or sinew (and remove most of the fat) before grinding. It's also best to use well-chilled meat for grinding, because it is firmer and will be easier to grind. Some manufacturers also recommend chilling the meat in the freezer for a short time (30 minutes or so) before grinding.

As a general guide, for ground beef, suitable cuts include skirt, flank, chuck, shoulder, or blade, round, or sirloin steak. For ground lamb, suitable cuts include shoulder and breast. For ground pork, suitable cuts include leg and lean belly, and for ground venison, suitable cuts include flank and shoulder.

If you use leaner cuts of meat, you may need to add some meat fat or a percentage of fattier meat so that the ground meat doesn't dry out too much during cooking. A little fat also adds flavor as well as juiciness to the cooked meat, especially when making recipes such as burgers.

Before you begin, cut the meat into small chunks or cubes (about 1 inch) to make it easier to grind more quickly, easily, and uniformly.

Grind the meat in batches. Once ground, either use the meat immediately or store it in a covered or airtight container in the refrigerator and use within one or two days.

To prepare your own ground chicken or turkey, use skinless, boneless chicken breasts or turkey breast cutlets, or boneless thigh meat. Remove any tendons or pieces of fat, then cut the meat into 1-inch cubes. Either use a meat grinder to grind the chicken or turkey, or place it in a food processor and pulse in short bursts until the meat is finely or coarsely chopped, depending on your requirements; do not overprocess the meat. Once ground, use immediately or store as above.

Always wash your hands thoroughly before and after handling raw (or cooked) meat or poultry. Once you have finished grinding your meat, take the grinder apart and wash it thoroughly in hot, soapy water, then carefully dry it as best you can, and let the parts air-dry completely before storing. Make sure work surfaces and all other utensils used are also cleaned with hot, soapy water, and disinfect worktops after use, preferably with a mild detergent or an antibacterial cleaner.

# BEEF & PEA SOUP

**SERVES: 6**       **PREP TIME: 20 MINS**       **COOK TIME: 40 MINS**

## INGREDIENTS

2 tablespoons vegetable oil
1 large onion, finely chopped
2 garlic cloves, finely chopped
1 green bell pepper,
seeded and sliced
2 carrots, sliced
1 (15-ounce) can
black-eyed peas
8 ounces ground beef
1 teaspoon each ground cumin,
chili powder, and paprika
¼ cabbage, sliced
2 tomatoes, peeled and
chopped
2½ cups beef stock
salt and pepper, to taste

**1.** Heat the oil in a large saucepan over medium heat. Add the onion and garlic and cook, stirring frequently, for 5 minutes, or until softened. Add the bell pepper and carrots and cook for an additional 5 minutes.

**2.** Meanwhile, drain the peas, reserving the liquid from the can. Place two-thirds of the peas, reserving the remainder, in a food processor or blender with the pea liquid and process until smooth.

**3.** Add the beef to the saucepan and cook, stirring constantly, to break up any lumps, until well browned. Add the spices and cook, stirring, for 2 minutes. Add the cabbage, tomatoes, stock, and pureed peas and season with salt and pepper. Bring to a boil, then reduce the heat, cover, and simmer for 15 minutes, or until the vegetables are tender.

**4.** Stir in the reserved peas, cover, and simmer for an additional 5 minutes. Ladle the soup into warm bowls and serve immediately.

# MEAL-IN-A-BOWL BEEF & HERB SOUP

**SERVES: 6**          **PREP TIME: 10 MINS**          **COOK TIME: APPROX. 1 HR**

## INGREDIENTS

2 onions

2 tablespoons sunflower oil

1 tablespoon ground turmeric

1 teaspoon ground cumin

½ cup dried green or yellow split peas

5 cups beef stock

8 ounces ground beef

1 cup long-grain rice

1 tablespoon chopped fresh cilantro, plus extra to garnish

1 tablespoon snipped fresh chives

1 cup finely chopped baby spinach

2 tablespoons butter

2 garlic cloves, finely chopped

3 tablespoons chopped fresh mint

salt and pepper, to taste

Greek-style yogurt, to serve

1. Grate one of the onions into a bowl and finely chop the other. Heat the oil in a large saucepan. Add the chopped onion and cook over low–medium heat, stirring occasionally, for 8–10 minutes, until golden. Stir in the turmeric and cumin, add the split peas, and pour in the stock. Bring to a boil, then reduce the heat, cover, and simmer for 15 minutes.

2. Meanwhile, add the beef to the grated onion, season with salt and pepper, and mix well. Shape the mixture into small balls.

3. Add the meatballs to the soup, replace then lid, and simmer for an additional 10 minutes. Add the rice and stir in the cilantro, chives, and spinach. Simmer, stirring frequently, for 25–30 minutes, until the rice is tender.

4. Melt the butter in a skillet. Add the garlic and cook over low heat, stirring frequently, for 2–3 minutes. Stir in the mint and cook for an additional minute.

5. Transfer the soup to warm bowls and sprinkle with the garlic mixture. Serve immediately with Greek-style yogurt and garnished with cilantro.

# MEATLOAF

There are many versions of this well-loved comfort food.
This one uses a glaze that is not only delicious but also helps
keep the meat wonderfully moist.

**SERVES: 6–8**

**PREP TIME: 20 MINS
PLUS RESTING**

**COOK TIME:
APPROX. 1½ HRS**

## INGREDIENTS

2 tablespoons butter

1 tablespoon olive oil, plus
extra for brushing

3 garlic cloves, chopped

2 carrots, finely diced

1 large celery stalk, finely diced

1 onion, finely diced

1 red bell pepper, seeded and
finely diced

4 large white mushrooms,
finely diced

1 teaspoon dried thyme

2 teaspoons finely chopped
rosemary

1 teaspoon Worcestershire
sauce

⅓ cup ketchup

½ teaspoon cayenne pepper

2½ pounds ground beef, chilled

2 eggs, beaten

1 cup fresh bread crumbs

2 tablespoons packed
light brown sugar

1 tablespoon Dijon mustard

salt and pepper, to taste

**1.** Melt the butter with the oil and garlic in a large
skillet. Add the vegetables and mushrooms and
cook over medium heat, stirring frequently, for 10
minutes, until most of the moisture has evaporated.

**2.** Remove from the heat and stir in the herbs,
Worcestershire sauce, ¼ cup of the ketchup, and the
cayenne pepper. Let cool.

**3.** Preheat the oven to 325°F. Brush a 9-inch loaf pan
with oil.

**4.** Put the beef into a large bowl and gently break
it up with your fingertips. Add the vegetable
mixture and eggs, season with salt and pepper,
and mix gently with your fingers. Add the bread
crumbs and mix.

**5.** Transfer the meatloaf mixture to the loaf pan.
Smooth the surface and bake in the preheated
oven for 30 minutes.

**6.** Meanwhile, make a glaze by whisking together
the sugar, the remaining 2 tablespoons of ketchup,
mustard, and a pinch of salt.

**7.** Remove the meatloaf from the oven and spread the glaze evenly over the top. Return to the oven and bake for an additional 35–45 minutes. To check that the meatloaf is cooked through, cut into the middle to make sure the meat is no longer pink. Any juices that run out should be clear and piping hot, with visible steam rising.

**8.** Remove from the oven and let rest for at least 15 minutes. Slice thickly to serve.

# HAMBURGERS

Burgers now come in many different flavorings, shapes, and sizes with something to suit all palettes. This classic recipe uses just a small amount of chile and a sprig of fresh basil to add an extra taste sensation.

**MAKES: 4**          **PREP TIME: 20 MINS**          **COOK TIME: 10–20 MINS**

## INGREDIENTS

1½ pounds ground beef
1 red bell pepper, seeded and finely chopped
1 garlic clove, finely chopped
2 small red chiles, seeded and finely chopped
1 tablespoon chopped fresh basil
½ teaspoon ground cumin
salt and pepper, to taste
fresh basil sprigs, to garnish
burger buns, halved, to serve

1. Preheat the broiler to medium–high. Put the beef, red bell pepper, garlic, chiles, chopped basil, and cumin into a bowl.

2. Mix until well combined and season with salt and pepper.

3. Using your hands, form the mixture into four patties. Place the patties under the preheated broiler and cook for 5–8 minutes.

4. Using a spatula, turn the burgers and cook on the other side for 5–8 minutes. To make sure the burgers are cooked through, cut into the middle to check that the meat is no longer pink. Any juices that run out should be clear and piping hot with steam rising.

5. Garnish with basil sprigs and serve immediately in burger buns.

**HERO TIPS** Always handle the ground beef gently when shaping your patties. Overworking the meat will result in a tougher—and much less enjoyable—hamburger.

# GROUND BEEF PIZZA

**SERVES: 2**          **PREP TIME: 20 MINS**          **COOK TIME: APPROX. 30 MINS**

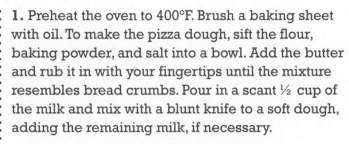

## INGREDIENTS

olive oil, for brushing and drizzling

8 ounces ground beef

1 small onion, finely chopped

1 garlic clove, finely chopped

1 teaspoon ground cumin

¼ cup drained and finely chopped chargrilled red pepper from a jar

1 tablespoon chopped fresh cilantro

¼ cup tomato paste

14 ounces mozzarella cheese, sliced

salt and pepper, to taste

## PIZZA DOUGH

1⅓ cups all-purpose flour, plus extra for dusting

¼ teaspoon baking powder

pinch of salt

2 tablespoons butter, cut into small pieces

about ½ cup milk

**1.** Preheat the oven to 400°F. Brush a baking sheet with oil. To make the pizza dough, sift the flour, baking powder, and salt into a bowl. Add the butter and rub it in with your fingertips until the mixture resembles bread crumbs. Pour in a scant ½ cup of the milk and mix with a blunt knife to a soft dough, adding the remaining milk, if necessary.

**2.** Turn out the dough onto a lightly floured surface and knead gently. Roll out to a 10-inch circle and transfer to the prepared baking sheet. Push up the edge slightly all around to make a rim.

**3.** Put the beef, onion, garlic, and cumin in a nonstick skillet and cook over medium heat, stirring frequently and breaking up the meat with a wooden spoon, for 5–8 minutes, until evenly browned. Stir in the red pepper and cilantro and season with salt and pepper.

**4.** Spread the tomato paste over the pizza crust. Cover with the beef mixture, top with the mozzarella, and drizzle with oil. Bake in the preheated oven for 15–20 minutes, until the crust is crisp. Serve immediately.

# BEEF FRIED RICE

**SERVES: 6**     **PREP TIME: 5 MINS**     **COOK TIME: 25–30 MINS**

## INGREDIENTS

2½ cups long-grain rice
2 tablespoons peanut oil
4 extra-large eggs, lightly beaten
1½ pounds ground beef
1 large onion, finely chopped
2 garlic cloves, finely chopped
1 cup frozen peas
3 tablespoons light soy sauce
1 teaspoon sugar
salt, to taste

**1.** Cook the rice in a large saucepan of salted boiling water for 15 minutes, or according to the package directions, until tender. Drain the rice, rinse with boiling water, and set aside.

**2.** Heat a wok over medium heat, then add the peanut oil, swirl it around the wok, and heat. Add the eggs and cook, stirring constantly, for 50–60 seconds, until set. Transfer to a dish and set aside.

**3.** Add the beef to the wok and stir-fry, breaking it up with a wooden spoon, for 4–5 minutes, until evenly browned. Stir in the onion, garlic, and peas and stir-fry for an additional 3–4 minutes.

**4.** Add the rice, soy sauce, sugar, and eggs and cook, stirring constantly, for another 1–2 minutes, until heated through. Serve immediately.

**HERO TIPS**

This dish is perfect for using leftover rice. You can also use any meat and vegetables on hand, making it the ideal staples meal.

# PORK & ROSEMARY BURGERS

A quick-and-easy alternative to the classic hamburger, this tasty pork version is beautifully flavored with garlic and rosemary and makes for a fantastic treat any day of the week.

**MAKES: 4**　　**PREP TIME: 10 MINS**　　**COOK TIME: APPROX. 10 MINS**

## INGREDIENTS

1 pound ground pork
1 small onion, finely chopped
1 garlic clove, crushed
1 tablespoon finely chopped fresh rosemary
oil, for brushing
1 small French bread, halved lengthwise and cut into four
2 tomatoes, sliced
4 pickles, sliced
¼ cup Greek-style yogurt
2 tablespoons chopped fresh mint
salt and pepper, to taste

**1.** Add the pork, onion, garlic, and rosemary to a large mixing bowl, season with salt and pepper, and use your hands to mix together.

**2.** Divide the mixture into four and shape into flat patties.

**3.** Brush a ridged grill pan or skillet with oil and cook the patties for 6–8 minutes, turning once, until golden and cooked through.

**4.** Place a burger on the bottom half of each piece of French bread and top with the tomatoes and pickles. Mix together the yogurt and mint.

**5.** Spoon the minty yogurt over the burgers and replace the bread tops to serve.

# PORK-STUFFED FLATBREADS

Ground allspice, cumin, and coriander capture the warming flavors of the Middle East with these simple flatbreads. This recipe uses the classic thin, round flatbreads, but it works equally well with warm pita breads.

**SERVES: 4**

**PREP TIME: 10 MINS PLUS STANDING**

**COOK TIME: 20 MINS**

## INGREDIENTS

1 red onion, halved and thinly sliced

2 tablespoons olive oil

1 pound ground pork

1 yellow onion, finely chopped

2 garlic cloves, finely chopped

1 tablespoon tomato paste

1 teaspoon ground allspice

1 teaspoon ground coriander

1 teaspoon ground cumin

¼ teaspoon crushed red pepper flakes, or to taste

1 cup drained and crumbled feta cheese

2 tablespoons chopped fresh cilantro

salt and pepper, to taste

## TO SERVE

8 flatbreads

sliced pickled chiles

Greek-style yogurt (optional)

**1.** Put the red onion into a nonmetallic bowl, sprinkle with salt, and set aside for 20 minutes to soften. Rinse well, then squeeze dry and set aside.

**2.** Heat the oil in a skillet over medium heat. Add the pork and yellow onion and sauté, stirring to break up the meat, for 5 minutes, or until the pork is brown. Spoon off any excess fat.

**3.** Add the garlic, tomato paste, spices, red pepper flakes, season with salt and pepper, and stir for 1–3 minutes, until the pork is cooked through. Stir in the cheese and chopped cilantro.

**4.** Place the flatbreads, one at a time, in a large skillet over medium–high heat and heat until warmed through. Place one-eighth of the filling along the center and top with the red onions, pickled chiles, and a dollop of yogurt, if using.

**5.** Fold the flatbreads in half, then cut each one in half. Serve immediately while still warm.

# MEATBALL RISOTTO

**SERVES: 4**

**PREP TIME: 20 MINS PLUS SOAKING**

**COOK TIME: 1 HR 15 MINS**

## INGREDIENTS

1 thick slice white bread, crusts removed

water or milk, for soaking

1 pound ground pork

2 garlic cloves, minced

1 tablespoon finely chopped onion

1 teaspoon black peppercorns, lightly crushed

pinch of salt

1 egg, lightly beaten

canola oil, for pan-frying

1 (14½-ounce) can diced tomatoes

1 tablespoon tomato paste

1 teaspoon dried oregano

1 teaspoon fennel seeds

pinch of sugar

4 cups beef stock

1 tablespoon olive oil

3 tablespoons butter

1 small onion, finely chopped

1½ cups risotto rice

⅔ cup red wine

salt and pepper, to taste

fresh basil leaves, to garnish

**1.** Place the bread into a bowl, add the water, and let soak for 5 minutes. Squeeze out the water, put into a dry bowl along with the ground pork, garlic, onion, crushed peppercorns, and pinch of salt. Add the egg and mix thoroughly. Shape the mixture into 16 equal balls.

**2.** Heat the canola oil in a skillet over medium heat. Add the meatballs and cook for 5 minutes, or until cooked though. Remove and drain.

**3.** Combine the tomatoes, tomato paste, herbs, and sugar in a heavy saucepan. Add the meatballs and bring to a boil. Reduce the heat and simmer for 30 minutes.

**4.** Bring the stock to a boil in a saucepan, then reduce the heat and keep simmering gently over low heat while you are cooking the risotto.

**5.** Meanwhile, heat the olive oil with 2 tablespoons of the butter in a deep saucepan until the butter has melted. Stir in the onion and cook for 5 minutes, until golden.

**6.** Reduce the heat, add the rice, and mix to coat in oil and butter. Cook, stirring constantly, for 2–3 minutes, or until the grains are translucent. Add the wine and cook, stirring constantly until reduced.

**7.** Gradually add the simmering stock. Stir constantly and add more liquid as the rice absorbs each addition. Increase the heat so that the liquid simmers. Cook for 20 minutes. Season with salt and pepper.

**8.** Lift out the cooked meatballs and add to the risotto. Remove the risotto from the heat and add the remaining butter. Mix well. Divide the risotto and a few meatballs among four plates. Drizzle with the tomato sauce, garnish with the basil, and serve.

# LAMB & MASHED POTATO PIE

**SERVES: 6**   **PREP TIME: 10 MINS**   **COOK TIME: 1½ HRS**

## INGREDIENTS
### FILLING

1 tablespoon olive oil

2 onions, finely chopped

2 garlic cloves, finely chopped

1½ pounds ground lamb

2 carrots, finely chopped

1 tablespoon all-purpose flour

1 cup beef stock or chicken stock

½ cup red wine

Worcestershire sauce (optional)

salt and pepper, to taste

### MASHED POTATO TOPPING

6 Yukon gold or russet potatoes, peeled and cut into chunks

4 tablespoons butter

2 tablespoons cream or milk

**1.** Preheat the oven to 350°F. Heat the oil in a large flameproof casserole dish and sauté the onions until softened, then add the garlic and stir well. Increase the heat and add the meat. Cook quickly to brown the meat all over, stirring continuously. Add the carrots and season well. Stir in the flour and add the stock and wine. Stir well and heat until simmering and thickened.

**2.** Cover the casserole dish and bake in the preheated oven for 1 hour. Check the consistency from time to time and add a little more stock or wine, if required. The meat mixture should be thick but not dry. Season with salt and pepper and add a little Worcestershire sauce, if using.

**3.** Meanwhile, make the mashed potato topping. Bring a large saucepan of lightly salted water to a boil, add the potatoes, and cook for 15–20 minutes. Drain well and mash with a potato masher until smooth. Season with salt and pepper and add the butter and cream, stirring until smooth.

**4.** Spoon the lamb mixture into an ovenproof dish and spread or pipe the potato on top. Increase the oven temperature to 400°F and bake at the top of the oven for an additional 15–20 minutes, until golden brown. Serve immediately.

# SPICE IT UP

# WHITE CHILI

White Chili uses ground chicken instead of beef and cannellini beans in place of red kidney beans. To keep the chicken tender, avoid breaking it up into small pieces in step 1. It doesn't need to be completely cooked at this stage, because it continues to cook later in the recipe.

**SERVES: 4**          **PREP TIME: 10 MINS**          **COOK TIME: 25 MINS**

## INGREDIENTS

2 tablespoons sunflower oil

1 pound ground chicken

1 large onion, chopped

2 large garlic cloves, finely chopped

2 teaspoon dried oregano

1 teaspoon dried thyme

1 teaspoon ground coriander

1 teaspoon ground cumin

½ teaspoon cayenne pepper, or to taste

1 (15-ounce) can cannellini beans, drained and rinsed

1 (14½-ounce) can diced tomatoes

½ cup tomato puree or tomato sauce

½ teaspoon packed light brown sugar

salt and pepper, to taste

finely chopped fresh flat-leaf parsley, to garnish

cooked long-grain rice and sour cream (optional), to serve

1. Heat the oil in a saucepan over medium–high heat. Add the chicken and onion and sauté, stirring with a wooden spoon to break up the meat into large clumps, for 3–5 minutes, until the onion is soft.

2. Add the garlic, oregano, thyme, coriander, cumin, and cayenne pepper and sauté for another minute.

3. Add the beans, tomatoes, tomato puree or sauce, and sugar, and season with salt and pepper. Bring to a boil, stirring. Reduce the heat to low, cover, and simmer for 10–15 minutes, until the chicken is completely cooked. Adjust the seasoning, if necessary.

4. Divide the rice among four bowls, spoon the chili over the top, and sprinkle with parsley. Serve immediately with sour cream on the side, if using.

# THAI CHICKEN PATTIES

**SERVES: 4**          **PREP TIME: 10 MINS**          **COOK TIME: APPROX. 20 MINS**

## INGREDIENTS

½ bunch scallions, trimmed and coarsely chopped

1¼ -inch piece fresh ginger, coarsely chopped

3 garlic cloves, crushed

handful fresh cilantro, including the stems

1 red chile, seeded and coarsely chopped

1 pound ground chicken

2 tablespoons light soy sauce

dash of Thai fish sauce

1 egg white

2 tablespoons all-purpose flour

finely grated zest of 1 lime

2–3 tablespoons vegetable oil, for frying

pepper, to taste

lime wedges and sweet chili sauce, to serve

**1.** Put the scallions, ginger, garlic, cilantro, and chile in a food processor or blender and process until everything is finely chopped.

**2.** Transfer to a mixing bowl, add the chicken along with the soy sauce, fish sauce, egg white, flour, and lime zest, season with black pepper, and combine.

**3.** Heat a little oil in a nonstick skillet and add spoonfuls of the mixture in batches. Cook each batch for about 4 minutes on each side, until golden and cooked through. Transfer to a plate and keep warm while cooking the remaining mixture.

**4.** Serve the cooked Thai chicken cakes with lime wedges and sweet chili sauce for dipping.

**HERO TIPS**

As well as creating these gorgeous little cakes, you can also shape them into much smaller balls and serve on toothpicks as a perfect dinner party appetizer.

# AROMATIC CHICKEN & COUSCOUS

**SERVES: 4**　　　　**PREP TIME: 5 MINS**　　　　**COOK TIME: APPROX. 30 MINS**

## INGREDIENTS

2 tablespoons vegetable oil

1 large onion, finely chopped

2 garlic cloves, finely chopped

1 tablespoon ground cumin

1 teaspoon ground cinnamon

2 teaspoons ground turmeric

1 pound ground chicken

2 cups chicken stock

½ cup raisins

1¼ cups couscous

finely grated rind and juice of 1 lemon

¼ cup pine nuts, toasted

salt and pepper, to taste

sprigs of fresh flat-leaf parsley, to garnish

**1.** Heat the oil in a large, nonstick skillet, add the onion, and cook over low heat, stirring occasionally, for 4–5 minutes, until softened. Add the garlic and spices and cook for an additional 1 minute over medium heat.

**2.** Add the chicken and cook, stirring frequently and breaking up the meat with a wooden spoon, for 4–5 minutes, until lightly browned. Add the stock and raisins, cover, and cook over low heat for an additional 8–10 minutes.

**3.** Add the couscous, season with salt and pepper, stir, and cover again. Simmer for 5–6 minutes, until the couscous has absorbed the stock and is completely cooked.

**4.** Remove from the heat, then stir in the lemon rind and juice and pine nuts. Garnish with parsley and serve immediately.

# SPICY TURKEY SLOPPY JOES

**MAKES: 4**            **PREP TIME: 10 MINS**            **COOK TIME: 25–30 MINS**

## INGREDIENTS

1½ tablespoons sunflower oil

1 celery stalk, finely chopped

1 onion, finely chopped

1 red bell pepper, seeded and finely chopped

1 pound fresh ground turkey

1 tablespoon all-purpose flour

½ teaspoon cayenne pepper, or to taste

1 teaspoon allspice

1 tablespoon dried parsley

1¾ cups canned cream of tomato soup

½ cup water

¼ cup ketchup

1 tablespoon Worcestershire sauce

salt and pepper, to taste

4 hamburger buns and potato chips (optional), to serve

1. Heat the oil in a saucepan over medium–high heat. Add the celery, onion, and red bell pepper and sauté, stirring, for 3–5 minutes, until soft. Add the turkey and continue cooking, stirring with a wooden spoon to break up the meat, for 2–3 minutes, or until the meat loses its raw appearance.

2. Sprinkle in the flour, cayenne pepper, allspice, and parsley and continue cooking and stirring for an additional minute.

3. Add the soup, water, ketchup, and Worcestershire sauce and season with salt and pepper. Add very little salt because the Worcestershire sauce is salty. Bring to a boil, stirring.

4. Reduce the heat to low and simmer, stirring occasionally, for 12–15 minutes, until the turkey is cooked through and the mixture is thickened, being careful that the mixture doesn't stick to the bottom of the pan. Adjust the seasoning, if necessary.

5. Halve and toast the hamburger buns, divide the mixture among them, and serve hot with potato chips on the side, if using.

# CREOLE TURKEY-STUFFED BELL PEPPERS

**MAKES: 4**

**PREP TIME: 15 MINS**

**COOK TIME: 50–55 MINS**

## INGREDIENTS

4 large red bell peppers

1 tablespoon sunflower oil, plus extra for greasing

2 ounces chorizo sausage, skinned and diced

12 ounces ground turkey

1 celery stalk, finely chopped

1 onion, finely chopped

1 small green bell pepper, seeded and finely chopped

½ cup instant long-grain rice

1 cup hot chicken stock or vegetable stock

¼ cup tomato puree or tomato sauce

2 tablespoons chopped fresh parsley or snipped chives

½ teaspoon hot pepper sauce, plus extra to serve

salt and pepper, to taste

salad greens, to serve

1. Preheat the oven to 425°F and grease a baking dish. Cut off the red bell pepper tops and remove the cores and seeds, then set the bell peppers and tops aside.

2. Heat the oil in a skillet over medium–high heat. Add the chorizo and cook for 1–2 minutes, until it gives off its oil. Transfer to a dish, using a slotted spoon, and set aside.

3. Pour off all but 2 tablespoons of oil from the skillet. Add the turkey, celery, onion, and green pepper and sauté, stirring with a wooden spoon to break up the turkey into large clumps, for 3–5 minutes, until the onion is soft. Stir in the rice.

4. Add the stock, tomato puree or sauce, parsley, and hot pepper sauce, and season with salt and pepper. Bring to a boil, stirring. Divide the mixture among the red peppers, then arrange them in the prepared dish, topped with their "lids." Carefully pour in boiling water to fill the dish up to 1 inch, then cover tightly with aluminum foil.

5. Bake in the preheated oven for 40–45 minutes, or until the peppers are tender. Serve hot or at room temperature, with salad greens and the chorizo.

# CHILI CON CARNE

This well-loved favorite is perfect for serving to friends for a causal dinner party. Although it is often accompanied by rice, it is just as delicious with tortilla chips or fresh crusty bread.

**SERVES: 6**          **PREP TIME: 5 MINS**          **COOK TIME: 1 HR 45 MINS**

## INGREDIENTS

2 tablespoons canola oil
2 onions, thinly sliced
2 garlic cloves, finely chopped
1½ pounds ground beef
¾ cup canned diced tomatoes
⅓ cup tomato paste
1 teaspoon ground cumin
1 teaspoon cayenne pepper
1 tablespoon chili powder
1 teaspoon dried oregano
1 bay leaf
1½ cups beef stock
1 (15-ounce) can red kidney beans, drained and rinsed
salt, to taste
cooked rice, to serve

**1.** Heat the oil in a large saucepan. Add the onions and garlic and cook over low heat, stirring occasionally, for 5 minutes, until softened. Add the beef, increase the heat to medium, and cook, stirring frequently and breaking it up with a wooden spoon, for 8–10 minutes, until evenly browned.

**2.** Stir in the tomatoes, tomato paste, cumin, cayenne pepper, chili powder, oregano, bay leaf, and stock, then season with salt and bring to a boil. Reduce the heat, cover, and simmer, stirring occasionally, for 1 hour.

**3.** Add the kidney beans, replace the lid, and simmer, stirring occasionally, for an additional 30 minutes. Remove and discard the bay leaf and serve immediately with rice.

# BEEF & EGG NOODLES

**SERVES: 6**     **PREP TIME: 10 MINS**     **COOK TIME: 15–20 MINS**

## INGREDIENTS

1 pound dried egg noodles

2 tablespoons toasted sesame oil

2 tablespoons peanut oil

1 onion, finely chopped

1½ pounds ground beef

1-inch piece fresh ginger, thinly sliced

1 fresh red chile, seeded and thinly sliced

1½ teaspoon five-spice powder

2 carrots, thinly sliced diagonally

1 red bell pepper, seeded and diced

1½ cups snow peas

1¾ cups bean sprouts

**1.** Cook the noodles in a saucepan of boiling water for 3–4 minutes, or cook according to the package directions, until tender. Transfer the noodles to a bowl, add 1 tablespoon of the toasted sesame oil, and toss to coat.

**2.** Heat a wok over medium heat, then add the peanut oil, swirl it around the wok, and heat. Add the onion and stir-fry for a few minutes, until softened. Add the beef and stir-fry, breaking it up with a wooden spoon, for 3–5 minutes, until evenly browned.

**3.** Stir in the ginger, chile, and five-spice powder and cook, stirring constantly, for 1 minute, then add the carrots, red bell pepper, and snow peas. Stir-fry for an additional 4 minutes.

**4.** Add the bean sprouts, the remaining sesame oil, and the noodles and stir-fry for an additional 2 minutes. Serve immediately.

2

3

# BEEF NACHOS

This quick and easy nacho dip is fabulously fiery and ideal for serving at parties, accompanied with a selection of mouthwatering toppings and tortilla chips for loading.

**SERVES: 4–6**     **PREP TIME: 10 MINS**     **COOK TIME: 20 MINS**

## INGREDIENTS

1 tablespoon extra virgin olive oil
1 pound ground beef
1 tablespoon smoked paprika
¾ cup frozen corn kernels
chipotle tomato sauce
3 cups chopped fresh cilantro
salt, to taste
tortilla chips, to serve

## SUGGESTED TOPPINGS

shredded cheddar cheese
sour cream
hot pepper sauce
shredded lettuce

1. In a large skillet, heat the oil over medium–high heat. Add the beef and sauté until browned, breaking it up with a wooden spoon, for about 5 minutes. Add the paprika and stir until evenly distributed and aromatic. Add the corn kernels and chipotle tomato sauce.

2. Bring to a simmer, then reduce the heat, partly cover the skillet, and simmer, stirring occasionally, for about 10 minutes, or until the beef is cooked through. Season with salt. Stir in the cilantro and spoon into bowls. Have your toppings ready and pass them around. Serve the dip immediately with tortilla chips and a selection of toppings.

**HERO TIPS**

Chipotle sauces are available in the supermarkets, but if you fail to find a suitable one, search online where you'll find many spicy variations.

# BEEF MEATBALLS WITH SICHUAN CHILI SAUCE

**SERVES: 4**

**PREP TIME: 20 MINS PLUS CHILLING**

**COOK TIME: 15 MINS**

## INGREDIENTS

1 pound ground beef

1½ teaspoons grated onion

¾-inch piece fresh ginger, squeezed in a garlic press

1 garlic clove, crushed

finely grated zest of ½ lemon

½ teaspoon salt

¼ teaspoon pepper

good pinch of red pepper flakes

1 egg, beaten

2 teaspoons toasted sesame oil

peanut oil, for frying

1 cup prepared Sichuan sweet chili sauce

squeeze of lemon juice

3 scallions, green parts included, shredded

1. Put the beef, onion, ginger, garlic, and lemon zest into a bowl and mix well with a fork. Add the salt, pepper, and red pepper flakes, then stir in the beaten egg and the sesame oil and mix well.

2. Divide the mixture into 20 walnut-size balls, rolling them in the palm of your hand until firm. Arrange on a plate, cover with plastic wrap, and chill for 30 minutes, or until you are ready to cook.

3. Add peanut oil to a wok to a depth of ½ inch. Heat to 350°F, or until a cube of bread browns in 30 seconds.

4. Add the meatballs and cook for 8–10 minutes, turning occasionally with tongs until brown and crusty. Remove from the wok and drain on paper towels. Transfer to a warm serving dish and keep warm.

5. Pour the chili sauce into a small saucepan and simmer for 2–3 minutes. Add the lemon juice. Pour the sauce over the beef meatballs, sprinkle with the scallions, and serve immediately.

# FRESHNESS FIRST

Fresh ground red meat, such as ground beef, should have a typical fresh-meat smell and an even pink or bright-or darker-red color (the depth of the pink/red color will depend on the type of meat). If the meat looks discolored (with a brown-gray, gray, or dark-brown color all the way through), if it feels tacky, sticky, or slimy, or if it has an "off" or sour odor, then it is probably spoiled and should be thrown away. If you are in any doubt about the freshness of the meat (be it ground red meat or ground chicken or turkey), discard it because it could contain harmful bacteria that may be dangerous to consume.

Darker, evenly colored ground red meat usually has a lower fat content than ground red meat that is paler or visibly streaked or flecked with white fat. The redder the ground meat, the less visible fat you will see. Choose ground red meat with a low or lower percentage of fat if you can (depending on the recipe you are preparing), and check the label for details of the typical fat content if you are buying from a supermarket or similar outlet. Ground pork and lamb can be fatty, so drain off the excess fat when cooking, or look for lean ground pork, if you prefer.

For some ground-meat recipes, however, the meat needs to include a certain amount of fat to give it moisture and flavor as it cooks. For example, choose ground chuck beef that has a higher fat content

when making recipes such as burgers; the fat will baste and flavor the burgers during cooking, keeping them succulent (some of the fat will drain away). Select lower-fat ground beef, such as ground round or sirloin, for recipes like chili con carne or a meat sauce for spaghetti.

The best place to buy ground meat is from a trusted supplier. Most good butchers will also be happy to grind fresh meat to order, so this enables you to choose a piece of meat and have it ground for you. Free-range or organic ground meat, including beef, lamb, pork, and ground turkey, is also obtainable, although it will probably be more expensive than standard ground meat.

# PORK MEATBALLS IN A CHILI BROTH

**SERVES: 4**

**PREP TIME: 20 MINS PLUS CHILLING**

**COOK TIME: 25 MINS**

## INGREDIENTS

5 cups chicken stock

¼–½ fresh red chile, seeded and finely sliced

½ teaspoon palm sugar or brown sugar

3 fresh thyme sprigs

2 lemongrass stalks, fibrous outer leaves removed, stems bashed with the flat of a knife

¼ teaspoon pepper

1 small head bok choy, stems cut into small squares, leaves sliced into ribbons

1 scallion, green parts included, sliced diagonally

dash of soy sauce

salt, to taste

## PORK MEATBALLS

8 ounces ground pork

1 shallot, grated

¾-inch piece fresh ginger, crushed

1 garlic clove, crushed

finely grated rind and juice of ½ lime

⅓ cup peanut oil

1. Pour the stock into a medium saucepan. Add the chile, sugar, thyme, lemongrass, and pepper, season with salt, and bring to a boil. Reduce the heat and simmer gently for 10 minutes. Remove from the heat and let cool for about 30 minutes.

2. To make the meatballs, combine the pork, shallot, ginger, garlic, lime rind, and juice and season. Mix well with a fork. Line a plate with paper towels.

3. Divide the mixture into 16–20 walnut-size balls. Place on the prepared plate and chill for 30 minutes.

4. Heat a large wok over high heat. Add the oil and heat until hot. Add the pork meatballs and cook for 5–6 minutes, until golden brown all over and cooked through. Drain on paper towels and keep warm.

5. Remove the thyme and lemongrass from the broth. Add the bok choy and scallion. Bring to a boil then simmer for 2 minutes, until the bok choy stems are just tender. Season with soy sauce.

6. Ladle the broth and vegetables over the meatballs and serve immediately.

# CHINESE BEEF & NOODLES

The traditional Chinese name for this dish is "ants climbing a tree." It comes from the effect of the tiny pieces of ground beef clinging to the noodles, which look like ants climbing on twigs.

**SERVES: 4**

**PREP TIME: 10 MINS PLUS MARINATING**

**COOK TIME: 6 MINS**

## INGREDIENTS

8 ounces thick rice noodles

1 tablespoon cornstarch

3 tablespoons soy sauce

1½ tablespoons Chinese rice wine

1½ teaspoons sugar

1½ teaspoons sesame oil

12 ounces lean ground beef

1½ tablespoons peanut oil

2 large garlic cloves, finely chopped

1 large fresh red chile, or to taste, seeded and thinly sliced

3 scallions, finely chopped

finely chopped fresh cilantro, to garnish

**1.** Cook the noodles according to the package directions, drain well, and set aside.

**2.** Meanwhile, put the cornstarch in a separate large bowl, then stir in the soy sauce, rice wine, sugar, and sesame oil, stirring until smooth. Add the ground beef and use your hands to toss the ingredients together without squeezing the meat. Set aside to marinate for 10 minutes.

**3.** Heat a wok over high heat, then add the peanut oil. Add the garlic, chile, and scallions and stir around for about 30 seconds. Add the ground beef together with any marinade left in the bowl and stir-fry for about 5 minutes, or until the beef is no longer pink. Add the noodles and use two forks to mix together. Sprinkle with the chopped cilantro and serve immediately.

# BEEF & LAMB SKEWERS

**MAKES: 4**

**PREP TIME: 15 MINS PLUS CHILLING**

**COOK TIME: 10 MINS**

## INGREDIENTS

8 ounces ground beef

4 ounces ground lamb

½ onion, grated

2 tablespoons chopped fresh flat-leaf parsley

1 tablespoon chopped fresh cilantro

1 garlic clove, minced

1 teaspoon ground cumin

¼ teaspoon ground cinnamon

½ teaspoon hot paprika, or to taste

½ teaspoon harissa paste, or to taste

½ teaspoon salt

pinch of cayenne pepper, or to taste

olive oil, for brushing

mixed salad and warm pita bread, to serve

**1.** Put the ground beef and lamb in a food processor and process to a paste. Add the onion, herbs, garlic, cumin, cinnamon, paprika, harissa paste, salt, and cayenne pepper and process again until blended.

**2.** Divide the mixture into four. Wrap the mixture around metal skewers to form oval shapes. Cover with plastic wrap and chill in the refrigerator for at least 1 hour, but ideally up to 4 hours.

**3.** Preheat the broiler. Brush the meat with a little oil and cook under the preheated broiler for 10 minutes, turning frequently, and brushing with more oil, if necessary, until cooked through.

**4.** Using a folded cloth to protect your fingers, hold the top of each skewer and use a fork to push the meat off. Serve with a mixed salad and warm pita bread.

# CHILI LAMB

This spicy lamb dish is certainly one for ringing the changes. Vary the fresh chilli and chili powder according to taste and serve with naan bread for scooping up every last tasty morsel.

**SERVES: 6**          **PREP TIME: 15 MINS**          **COOK TIME: 25–30 MINS**

## INGREDIENTS

2 tablespoons sunflower oil
1 onion, chopped
1 garlic clove, finely chopped
1 teaspoon grated fresh ginger
1 teaspoon ground coriander
½ teaspoon chili powder
¼ teaspoon ground turmeric
pinch of salt
12 ounces lean ground lamb
¾ cup canned diced tomatoes
1 tablespoon chopped fresh mint, plus extra sprigs to garnish
½ cup fresh or frozen peas
2 carrots, sliced into thin sticks
1 fresh green chile, seeded and finely chopped
1 tablespoon chopped fresh cilantro
naan or other flatbread, to serve

**1.** Heat the oil in a large, heavy skillet or Dutch oven. Add the onion and cook over low heat, stirring occasionally, for 10 minutes, or until golden.

**2.** Meanwhile, place the garlic, ginger, ground coriander, chili powder, turmeric, and salt in a small bowl and mix well. Add the spice mixture to the pan and cook, stirring constantly, for 2 minutes. Add the lamb and cook, stirring frequently and breaking up the lamb with a wooden spoon, for 8–10 minutes, or until browned all over.

**3.** Add the tomatoes, chopped mint, peas, carrots, chile, and chopped cilantro. Cook, stirring constantly, for 3–5 minutes. Garnish with mint sprigs and serve immediately with naan.

# PASTA PARTNERS

# CHICKEN MEATBALL PASTA

Chicken meatballs provide a much lighter and more delicately flavored alternative to the classic beef version. However, they are just as delicious and every bit as filling.

**SERVES: 4**  **PREP TIME: 15 MINS**  **COOK TIME: 35 MINS**

## INGREDIENTS

3 tablespoons olive oil
1 red onion, chopped
1 pound skinless, boneless chicken breasts, chopped
1 cup fresh white bread crumbs
2 teaspoons dried oregano
1 garlic clove, crushed
1 (14½-ounce) can diced tomatoes
1 tablespoon tomato paste
1¼ cups water
8 ounces dried spaghetti or linguine
salt and pepper, to taste
Parmesan cheese shavings, to serve

**1.** Heat 1 tablespoon of the oil in a large skillet and sauté half the chopped onion for 5 minutes, until just softened. Let cool.

**2.** Put the chicken, bread crumbs, oregano, and the sautéed onion in a food processor or blender. Season well with salt and pepper and process for 2–3 minutes, until thoroughly combined. Shape into 24 meatballs.

**3.** Heat the remaining oil in the skillet and cook the meatballs over medium–high heat for 3–4 minutes, until golden brown. Remove and set aside.

**4.** Add the remaining onion and the garlic to the pan and sauté for 5 minutes. Stir in the tomatoes, tomato paste, and water, and bring to a boil. Add the meatballs and simmer for 20 minutes. Season with salt and pepper.

**5.** Meanwhile, bring a large saucepan of lightly salted water to a boil. Add the pasta, bring back to a boil, and cook for 8–10 minutes, or according to package directions, until tender but still firm to the bite. Drain and toss with the meatballs and sauce. Serve immediately with Parmesan cheese shavings.

# CHICKEN & MUSHROOM LASAGNA

**SERVES: 4–6**          **PREP TIME: 15 MINS**          **COOK TIME: 1½ HRS**

## INGREDIENTS

2 tablespoons olive oil

1 large onion, finely chopped

1 pound ground chicken or ground turkey

4 ounces smoked pancetta, chopped

3½ cups chopped cremini mushrooms

4 ounces dried porcini, soaked

⅔ cup dry white wine

1 (14½-ounce) can diced tomatoes

3 tablespoons chopped fresh basil leaves

9 oven-ready lasagna noodles

3 tablespoons finely grated Parmesan cheese

salt and pepper, to taste

## WHITE SAUCE

2½ cups milk

4 tablespoons butter

⅓ cup all-purpose flour

1 bay leaf

**1.** Preheat the oven to 375°F. For the white sauce, heat the milk, butter, flour, and bay leaf in a saucepan, whisking constantly, until smooth and thick. Season with salt and pepper, cover, and let stand.

**2.** Heat the oil in a large saucepan and sauté the onion, stirring, for 3–4 minutes. Add the chicken and pancetta and cook for 6–8 minutes. Stir in both types of mushrooms and cook for an additional 2–3 minutes.

**3.** Add the wine and bring to a boil. Pour in the tomatoes, cover, and simmer for 20 minutes. Stir in the basil.

**4.** Arrange three of the lasagna noodles in a rectangular ovenproof dish, then spoon over one-third of the meat sauce. Remove and discard the bay leaf from the white sauce. Spread one-third of the sauce over the meat. Repeat the layers twice more, finishing with a layer of the white sauce.

**5.** Sprinkle with the cheese and bake in the preheated oven for 35–40 minutes, until the topping is golden and bubbling. Serve immediately.

1

3

5

# CHICKEN & ORZO CASSEROLE

**SERVES: 4**  **PREP TIME: 15 MINS**  **COOK TIME: 40 MINS**

## INGREDIENTS

⅓ cup drained ricotta cheese

1 cup shredded mozzarella cheese

½ cup grated Gruyère cheese

4 ounces dried orzo pasta

2 tablespoons olive oil, plus extra for oiling and drizzling

1 large onion, finely chopped

1 pound ground chicken

4 large garlic cloves, finely chopped

1 tablespoon dried mixed herbs

2 cups tomato puree or tomato sauce

⅓ cup fine dried bread crumbs

salt and pepper, to taste

**1.** Preheat the oven to 425°F and oil a 1½-quart ovenproof serving dish. Beat together the ricotta cheese, mozzarella cheese, and half the Gruyère cheese in a large bowl and set aside.

**2.** Bring a saucepan of lightly salted water to a boil. Add the pasta, bring back to a boil, and cook for 2 minutes less than specified in the package directions.

**3.** Meanwhile, heat the oil in a skillet over medium–high heat. Add the onion and sauté, stirring, for 2–3 minutes, until soft. Add the chicken, garlic, and herbs, stirring with a wooden spoon to break up the chicken into large clumps, for about 2 minutes, until it loses its raw appearance. Stir in the tomato puree or sauce, season with salt and pepper, bring to a boil, then simmer for 10 minutes.

**4.** Drain the pasta and immediately transfer to the bowl with the cheese. Add the chicken mixture, stirring until the cheeses melt.

**5.** Pour into the prepared dish and smooth the surface. Combine the remaining Gruyère cheese with the bread crumbs and sprinkle it over the pasta, then drizzle with oil. Bake in the preheated oven for 20–25 minutes, until the top is golden brown and bubbling. Serve immediately.

# TURKEY & MUSHROOM CANNELLONI

**SERVES: 4**          **PREP TIME: 15 MINS**          **COOK TIME: 1¾ HRS**

## INGREDIENTS

butter, for greasing
2 tablespoons olive oil
2 garlic cloves, crushed
1 large onion, finely chopped
8 ounces wild mushrooms, sliced
12 ounces ground turkey
4 ounces prosciutto, diced
⅔ cup red wine
¾ cup canned diced tomatoes
1 tablespoon shredded fresh basil leaves
2 tablespoons tomato paste
10–12 dried cannelloni tubes
2½ cups White Sauce (see page 74)
1 cup freshly grated Parmesan cheese
salt and pepper, to taste

1. Preheat the oven to 375°F. Lightly grease a large ovenproof dish. Heat the oil in a heavy skillet. Add the garlic, onion, and mushrooms and cook over low heat, stirring frequently, for 8–10 minutes. Add the ground turkey and prosciutto and cook, stirring frequently, for 12 minutes, or until browned all over. Stir in the red wine, tomatoes, basil, and tomato paste, and cook for 4 minutes. Season with salt and pepper, then cover and simmer for 30 minutes. Uncover, stir, and simmer for 15 minutes.

2. Meanwhile, bring a large saucepan of lightly salted water to a boil. Add the cannelloni tubes, bring back to a boil, and cook for 8–10 minutes, or according to the package directions, until tender but still firm to the bite. Using a slotted spoon, transfer the cannelloni tubes to a plate and pat dry with paper towels.

3. Using a teaspoon, fill the cannelloni tubes with the turkey-and-mushroom mixture. Transfer to the dish. Pour the White Sauce over them to cover completely and sprinkle with the Parmesan cheese.

4. Bake in the preheated oven for 30 minutes, or until golden and bubbling. Serve immediately.

# TURKEY PASTA PESTO

All along the Italian Liguria coast, trattorias serve the regional specialty of long, thin pasta shapes called *trofie*, boiled new potatoes, and green beans, all tossed together with homemade pesto sauce. Here, ground turkey makes this a more substantial main dish.

**SERVES: 4**  **PREP TIME: 10 MINS**  **COOK TIME: 12 MINS**

## INGREDIENTS

6 ounces dried trofie pasta or thin penne pasta

4 ounces new potatoes, scrubbed and thinly sliced

1 cup fine green bean pieces (cut to the same length as the pasta)

2 tablespoons olive oil

1 pound ground turkey

2 large garlic cloves, crushed

½ cup pesto sauce

salt and pepper, to taste

freshly grated Parmesan cheese or pecorino cheese, to serve

**1.** Bring a large saucepan of water to a boil with 1 teaspoon of salt. Add the pasta, bring back to a boil, and cook for 12 minutes, or according to the package directions. Add the potatoes 7 minutes before the end of the cooking time, then add the beans 2 minutes later.

**2.** Meanwhile, heat the oil in a large skillet over medium–high heat. Add the turkey and sauté, stirring with a wooden spoon to break it up into large clumps, for about 5 minutes, until just starting to brown. Add the garlic and sauté for an additional minute, or until the turkey is cooked through. Remove from the skillet and keep hot.

**3.** When the pasta and vegetables are tender, drain, reserving a few tablespoons of the cooking water. Return the pasta and vegetables to the pan, add the turkey and pesto, and toss together well. Add a little of the reserved cooking water, if necessary. Season with salt and pepper.

**4.** Divide the mixture among warm bowls and serve immediately, with plenty of cheese for sprinkling over the pasta.

# TURKEY STROGANOFF

## INGREDIENTS

3 tablespoons sunflower oil
1 pound ground turkey
2 tablespoons butter
1 onion, minced
2 large garlic cloves, minced
3½ cups thinly chopped cremini mushrooms
4 teaspoons Dijon mustard
freshly grated nutmeg, to taste
2 cups sour cream
freshly squeezed lemon juice, to taste
salt and pepper, to taste
finely chopped fresh flat-leaf parsley and cooked tagliatelle, to serve

1. Heat the oil in a large skillet over medium–high heat. Add the turkey and sauté, stirring with a wooden spoon to break up the meat into large clumps, for 4–6 minutes, until cooked through. Remove from the pan with a slotted spoon and set aside.

2. Pour off all but 1 tablespoon of the fat remaining in the skillet. Add the butter and heat until melted. Add the onion and sauté, stirring, for 3–5 minutes, until soft. Stir in the garlic and mushrooms and season with salt and pepper. Sauté, stirring, for about 5 minutes, until the mushrooms reabsorb the liquid they release.

3. Stir in the mustard and nutmeg, then return the turkey to the skillet. Stir in the sour cream and bring to a boil, stirring. Reduce the heat and simmer for a few minutes, until slightly reduced. Add lemon juice to taste and adjust the seasoning, if necessary.

4. Divide the pasta among four plates and pour the sauce over the top. Sprinkle with parsley and serve immediately.

# MEATY TOMATO SAUCE

**SERVES: 4**

**PREP TIME: 10 MINS PLUS SOAKING**

**COOK TIME: 1¼ HRS**

## INGREDIENTS

1 ounce dried porcini
½ cup lukewarm water
1 tablespoon butter
2 ounces pancetta, diced
1 small onion, finely chopped
1 garlic clove, finely chopped
2 small carrots, finely diced
2 celery stalks, finely diced
12 ounces ground beef
1 pinch sugar
freshly grated nutmeg, to taste
1 tablespoon tomato paste
½ cup red wine
1 cup tomato puree
or tomato sauce
salt and pepper, to taste

**1.** Soak the porcini in the water for 20 minutes.

**2.** Melt the butter in a saucepan, add the pancetta, and cook.

**3.** Add the onion and garlic and sauté until the onion is translucent. Stir in the carrots and celery and cook for a few minutes, stirring frequently.

**4.** Add the beef and sauté, stirring constantly. Season with salt and pepper, the sugar, and some nutmeg. Stir in the tomato paste and cook for a minute or two, then add the wine. Mix in the tomato puree or sauce. Thinly slice the porcini and add to the sauce. Pour the soaking water through a fine strainer into the sauce. Thicken the sauce by cooking it over low heat for 1 hour.

Spaghetti is the most suitable partner to go with this rich sauce but any pasta would be delicious. Alternatively, simply serve with rice or fresh bread.

# SPAGHETTI & MEATBALLS

This famous Italian-American dish is a favorite with adults and children alike. This version uses smaller meatballs but you can have fewer—but much larger—meatballs, if you prefer.

**SERVES: 4**        **PREP TIME: 25 MINS**        **COOK TIME: 35 MINS**

## INGREDIENTS

1 tablespoon olive oil
1 small onion, finely chopped
2 garlic cloves, finely chopped
2 fresh thyme sprigs, finely chopped
1½ pounds ground beef
½ cup fresh bread crumbs
1 egg, lightly beaten
1 pound dried spaghetti
salt and pepper, to taste

## SAUCE

1 onion, cut into wedges
3 red bell peppers, halved and seeded
1 (14½-ounce) can diced tomatoes
1 bay leaf
salt and pepper, to taste

**1.** Heat the oil in a skillet. Add the chopped onion and garlic and cook over low heat for 5 minutes, until softened. Remove from the heat and transfer the mixture to a bowl with the thyme, beef, bread crumbs, and egg. Season with salt and pepper and mix well. Shape into 20 meatballs.

**2.** Heat a large nonstick skillet over low–medium heat. Add the meatballs and cook, stirring gently and turning frequently, for 15 minutes, until lightly browned all over.

**3.** Meanwhile, preheat the broiler. Put the onion wedges and bell pepper halves, skin side up, on a broiler rack and cook under the preheated broiler, turning frequently, for 10 minutes, until the bell pepper skins are blistered and charred. Put the peppers into a plastic bag, tie the top, and let cool. Set the onion wedges aside.

**4.** Peel off the pepper skins. Coarsely chop the flesh and put it into a food processor or blender with the onion wedges and tomatoes. Process to a smooth puree and season with salt and pepper. Pour into a saucepan with the bay leaf and bring to a boil. Reduce the heat and simmer, stirring occasionally, for 10 minutes. Remove and discard the bay leaf.

**5.** Meanwhile, bring a saucepan of salted water to a boil. Add the spaghetti, return to a boil, and cook for 8–10 minutes, or according to package directions, until tender but still firm to the bite. Drain the spaghetti and serve immediately with the meatballs and sauce.

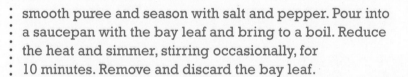

# TRADITIONAL LASAGNA

Many countries have their own version of this Italian classic. This lasagna omits any white sauce but instead opts for layers of Parmesan cheese before the whole dish is smothered with diced tomatoes.

**SERVES: 4**    **PREP TIME: 15 MINS**    **COOK TIME: 1¾ HRS PLUS STANDING**

## INGREDIENTS

2 tablespoons olive oil

2 ounces pancetta or bacon, chopped

1 garlic clove, finely chopped

1 onion, chopped

8 ounces ground beef

2 carrots, chopped

2 celery stalks, chopped

2 cups chopped mushrooms

pinch of dried oregano

⅓ cup red wine

⅔ cup beef stock

1 tablespoon tomato paste

8 ounces oven-ready lasagna noodles

1½ cups grated Parmesan cheese

1 (14½-ounce) can diced tomatoes

few fresh basil leaves, torn

salt and pepper, to taste

mixed salad, to serve

**1.** Heat the oil in a large saucepan. Add the pancetta and cook over medium heat, stirring occasionally, for 2–3 minutes. Reduce the heat to low, add the garlic and onion, and cook, stirring occasionally, for 5 minutes, until softened.

**2.** Add the beef, increase the heat to medium, and cook, stirring frequently and breaking it up with a wooden spoon, for 8–10 minutes, until evenly browned. Stir in the carrots, celery, and mushrooms and cook, stirring occasionally, for an additional 5 minutes. Add the oregano, pour in the wine and stock, and stir in the tomato paste. Season with salt and pepper. Bring to a boil, reduce the heat, and simmer for 40 minutes.

**3.** Preheat the oven to 375°F. Make alternating layers of the beef sauce, lasagna noodles, and Parmesan in a large, rectangular ovenproof dish. Pour the tomatoes over the top to cover completely. Bake in the preheated oven for 30 minutes. Remove the dish from the oven and let stand for 10 minutes, then sprinkle with torn basil, cut into four, and serve with a mixed salad.

# MEATY MACARONI & CHEESE

Give this student staple a twist by adding ground beef to create a hearty, filling meal. After trying this tasty remix, you may even be reluctant to go back to the classic meat-free version!

**SERVES: 4**       **PREP TIME: 15 MINS**       **COOK TIME: 1 HR 15 MINS**

## INGREDIENTS

2 tablespoons olive oil
1 onion, chopped
1 garlic clove, finely chopped
1 pound ground beef
1⅓ cups drained canned corn kernels
1 (14½-ounce) can diced tomatoes
1 teaspoon dried mixed herbs
8 ounces dried macaroni
3 tablespoons butter
⅓ cup all-purpose flour
2 cups milk
2 teaspoons Dijon mustard
1⅔ cups shredded Monterey Jack, American, or cheddar cheese
salt and pepper, to taste

**1.** Heat the oil in a saucepan. Add the onion and garlic and cook over low heat, stirring occasionally, for 5 minutes, until softened. Add the beef, increase the heat to medium, and cook, breaking it up with a wooden spoon, for 8–10 minutes, until lightly browned all over. Stir in the corn, tomatoes, and mixed herbs and season with salt and pepper. Reduce the heat, cover, and simmer, stirring occasionally, for 25–30 minutes.

**2.** Bring a large saucepan of salted water to a boil. Add the macaroni, return to a boil, and cook for 10 minutes, until tender but still firm to the bite.

**3.** Meanwhile, preheat the broiler. Melt the butter in a separate saucepan. Sprinkle in the flour and cook, stirring constantly, for 2 minutes. Remove the pan from the heat and gradually stir in the milk, a little at a time. Return the pan to the heat and bring to a boil, stirring constantly. Reduce the heat and simmer the sauce, stirring constantly, for 5 minutes, until thickened and smooth. Remove the pan from the heat and stir in the mustard and 1½ cups of the cheese. Stir well until the cheese has melted.

**4.** Drain the macaroni and add to the cheese sauce, stirring well to mix. Spoon the beef mixture into a baking dish, then cover with the macaroni mixture. Sprinkle with the remaining cheese and cook under the preheated broiler for 4–5 minutes, until the top is golden and bubbling. Serve immediately.

# ONE-DISH BEEF & PASTA

**SERVES: 4**          **PREP TIME: 15 MINS**          **COOK TIME: 30-40 MINS**

## INGREDIENTS

2 tablespoons olive oil

1 onion, chopped

1 garlic clove, finely chopped

1 celery stalk, chopped

1 carrot, chopped

1 pound lean ground beef

2 cups sliced white button mushrooms

1 (14½-ounce) can diced tomatoes

1 tablespoon tomato paste

1 teaspoon sugar

pinch of dried oregano

1 tablespoon chopped fresh flat-leaf parsley

6 ounces dried fusilli

¾ cup red wine

1½ tablespoons concentrated beef stock or 1 beef bouillon cube

salt and pepper, to taste

**1.** Heat the oil in a large saucepan with a tight-fitting lid. Add the onion, garlic, celery, and carrot and cook over low heat, stirring occasionally, for 5 minutes, until softened. Add the beef, increase the heat to medium, and cook, stirring frequently and breaking up the beef with a wooden spoon, for 5–8 minutes, until evenly browned.

**2.** Add the mushrooms and cook for an additional 3–4 minutes. Add the tomatoes, tomato paste, sugar, herbs, pasta, and wine. Stir in the concentrated stock, add just enough water to cover, and stir well.

**3.** Reduce the heat, cover tightly, and simmer gently for 15–20 minutes, until the pasta is tender but still firm to the bite and the sauce has thickened. Season with salt and pepper. Serve immediately.

# STORE YOUR KNOWLEDGE

Due to the large surface area of ground meat, it tends to have a shorter shelf life than most other fresh meats. Once ground or minced, meat begins to lose quality and flavor, so it should be used quickly and should always be cooked until well done. If you are grinding or mincing your own meat, then ideally prepare it just before you plan to use it.

Ground meat should be stored in a covered or airtight container (so that any juices don't drip and contaminate other foods) in the bottom of the refrigerator and should be eaten within one or two days, or check the expiration date, if it's provided on the packaging. If you buy ground meat from a supermarket or similar outlet, you can store it in its original packaging (some ground meat comes in vacuum packs), as long as it is airtight and sealed.

Ground meat should be frozen on the day of purchase and used within one month. Frozen ground meat should be thawed thoroughly in the refrigerator overnight (in a dish to catch any juices) before use. It should then be cooked as soon as possible, within 24 hours. Do not refreeze thawed ground meat; however, you can freeze it again once it is cooked in recipes.

Chilled fresh textured vegetable protein should be stored in the refrigerator and used by the expiration date. Once opened, it should be kept in a covered or airtight container in the refrigerator and used within 24 hours. Chilled fresh textured vegetable protein can also be frozen on the day of purchase for up to three months. As with ground meat, do not refreeze thawed textured vegetable protein; however, you can freeze it again (for up to one month) once it is cooked. Already-frozen textured vegetable protein can be cooked from frozen or thawed before use, but check the packaging for guidelines.

# BAKED PORK & PASTA

**SERVES: 4**     **PREP TIME: 10 MINS**     **COOK TIME: 1¼ HRS**

## INGREDIENTS

2 tablespoons olive oil

1 onion, chopped

1 garlic clove, finely chopped

2 carrots, diced

2 ounces pancetta, chopped

2 cups chopped white button mushrooms

1 pound ground pork

½ cup dry white wine

¼ cup tomato puree or tomato sauce

¾ cup canned diced tomatoes

2 teaspoon chopped fresh sage, plus extra sprigs to garnish

8 ounces dried penne

5 ounces mozzarella cheese, diced

¼ cup freshly grated Parmesan cheese

1¼ cups White Sauce (see page 74)

salt and pepper, to taste

**1.** Preheat the oven to 400°F. Heat the oil in a large, heavy skillet. Add the onion, garlic, and carrots and cook over low heat, stirring occasionally, for 5 minutes, or until the onion has softened.

**2.** Add the pancetta and cook for 5 minutes. Add the chopped mushrooms and cook, stirring occasionally, for an additional 2 minutes. Add the pork and cook until the meat has browned. Stir in the wine, tomato puree or sauce, tomatoes, and chopped fresh sage. Season with salt and pepper, bring to a boil, then cover and simmer over low heat for 25–30 minutes.

**3.** Meanwhile, bring a large, heavy saucepan of lightly salted water to a boil. Add the pasta, return to a boil, and cook for 8–10 minutes, or until tender but still firm to the bite. Spoon the pork mixture into a large ovenproof dish. Stir the mozzarella cheese and half the Parmesan cheese into the White Sauce.

**4.** Drain the pasta and stir the sauce into it, then spoon it over the pork mixture. Sprinkle with the remaining Parmesan cheese and bake in the preheated oven for 25–30 minutes, or until golden brown. Serve immediately, garnished with sage sprigs.

# LAMB & MACARONI CASSEROLE

This recipe shares its origins with a traditional Greek dish made with lamb. It is delicious served hot or cold with a fresh side salad—or vegetables, if you prefer.

**SERVES: 4**

**PREP TIME: 10 MINS**

**COOK TIME: APPROX. 1 HR 40 MINS**

## INGREDIENTS

1 tablespoon olive oil
1 onion, chopped
2 garlic cloves, finely chopped
1 pound ground lamb
2 tablespoons tomato paste
2 tablespoons all-purpose flour
1¼ cups chicken stock
1 teaspoon ground cinnamon
4 ounces dried macaroni
2 beefsteak tomatoes, sliced
1¼ cups Greek yogurt
2 eggs, lightly beaten
salt and pepper, to taste
salad greens, to serve

1. Preheat the oven to 375°F. Heat the oil in a large, heavy skillet. Add the onion and garlic and cook over low heat, stirring occasionally, for 5 minutes, or until softened. Add the lamb and cook, breaking it up with a wooden spoon, until browned all over. Add the tomato paste and sprinkle in the flour. Cook, stirring, for 1 minute, then stir in the chicken stock. Season with salt and pepper and stir in the cinnamon. Bring to a boil, reduce the heat, cover, and cook for 25 minutes.

2. Meanwhile, bring a large, heavy saucepan of lightly salted water to a boil. Add the pasta, return to a boil, and cook for 8–10 minutes, or until tender but still firm to the bite.

3. Drain the pasta and stir into the lamb mixture. Spoon into a large ovenproof dish and arrange the tomato slices on top. Beat together the yogurt and eggs, then spoon over the lamb evenly. Bake in the preheated oven for 1 hour. Serve immediately with salad greens.

# TASTY APPETIZERS

# GROUND CHICKEN SKEWERS

**MAKES: 8**          **PREP TIME: 10 MINS**          **COOK TIME: 8-10 MINS**

## INGREDIENTS

1 pound ground chicken

1 onion, finely chopped

1 fresh red chile, seeded and chopped

2 tablespoons Thai red curry paste

1 teaspoon palm sugar or light brown sugar

1 teaspoon ground coriander

1 teaspoon ground cumin

1 egg white

8 lemongrass stalks

cooked rice with chopped scallion, to serve

cilantro sprigs, to garnish

**1.** Mix together the chicken, onion, chile, curry paste, and sugar in a bowl to a thick paste. Stir in the coriander, cumin, and egg white and mix again.

**2.** Preheat the broiler to high. Divide the mixture into eight equal portions and squeeze each one around a lemongrass stalk. Arrange on a broiler rack and cook under the preheated broiler, turning frequently, for 8 minutes, or until browned and cooked through. Serve immediately, accompanied by cooked rice with chopped scallion stirred through and garnished with the cilantro sprigs.

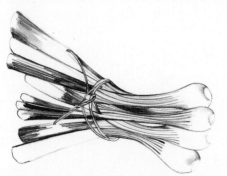

**HERO TIPS**

You can serve the skewers with a fresh salad and a dipping sauce. Try mixing dark soy sauce with a few crushed red pepper flakes, some ground ginger and garlic, and a splash of sesame oil.

# DIM SUM

These tasty little Cantonese bundles are traditionally served in small steamer baskets or on small plates and with tea—such as green tea or chrysanthemum tea.

**MAKES: 20–24**          **PREP TIME: 20 MINS**          **COOK TIME: 15–25 MINS**

## INGREDIENTS

12 ounces ground chicken

½ bunch scallions, trimmed and minced

2 tablespoons finely chopped fresh cilantro

1 tablespoon soy sauce

1 tablespoon grated fresh ginger

1 tablespoon rice wine vinegar

20–24 wonton wrappers

pepper, to taste

sweet chili sauce and dark soy sauce, to serve

**1.** Put the ground chicken, scallions, cilantro, soy sauce, ginger, and vinegar into a bowl and use a fork to combine. Season with pepper.

**2.** Place a teaspoon of the prepared filling in the center of each wonton wrapper. Use your fingers to rub the edges of the wrappers with warm water, gather the two opposite edges to form a tight seal, then bring together the remaining two sides in the middle at the top.

**3.** Cover the bottom of a bamboo steamer with a single layer of the dim sum. Or line the bottom of a steamer pan with some parchment paper and cover with the dim sum. Place over a saucepan of boiling water, cover, and steam for 7–8 minutes.

**4.** Remove from the steam and serve immediately with the chili sauce and soy sauce for dipping.

# MINI CHIMICHANGAS

**MAKES: ABOUT 10     PREP TIME: 20-25 MINS     COOK TIME: 25-30 MINS**

## INGREDIENTS

2 tablespoons vegetable oil, plus extra for frying

1 onion, finely chopped

8 ounces ground chicken

1 red chile, seeded and finely chopped

1 red bell pepper, seeded and minced

⅔ cup drained canned corn kernels

4 scallions, trimmed and finely chopped

¼ cup fresh tomato salsa

10 small flour tortillas

salt and pepper, to taste

**1.** Heat 2 tablespoons of the oil in a nonstick skillet, add the onion and ground chicken, and cook for 4–5 minutes, until the chicken starts to brown and the onion is soft.

**2.** Add the chile and red bell pepper and cook for an additional 2–3 minutes. Remove from the heat and stir in the corn, scallions, and salsa, season with salt and pepper, and put into a bowl. Wipe out the pan with paper towels.

**3.** Warm a tortilla briefly on each side in the skillet. Place a large spoonful of the filling in the center, fold in two sides of the tortilla, then the remaining two sides to form a small package. Secure with a wooden toothpick. Repeat with the remaining tortillas and filling.

**HERO TIPS**

If using a deep fryer be sure to fry only two or three chimichangas at a time as advised. Overcrowding the fryer will cause the oil temperature to drop and result in soggy packages.

**4.** Heat enough oil for frying in a skillet. Add two or three chimichangas and cook for 2 minutes, then turn and cook for an additional 2–3 minutes, until evenly golden brown. Alternatively, heat enough oil for deep-frying in a deep fryer to 350–375°F, or until a cube of bread browns in 30 seconds. Add two or three chimichangas and cook for 2–3 minutes, until golden brown. Drain on paper towels and keep warm while cooking the remaining chimichangas. Serve immediately.

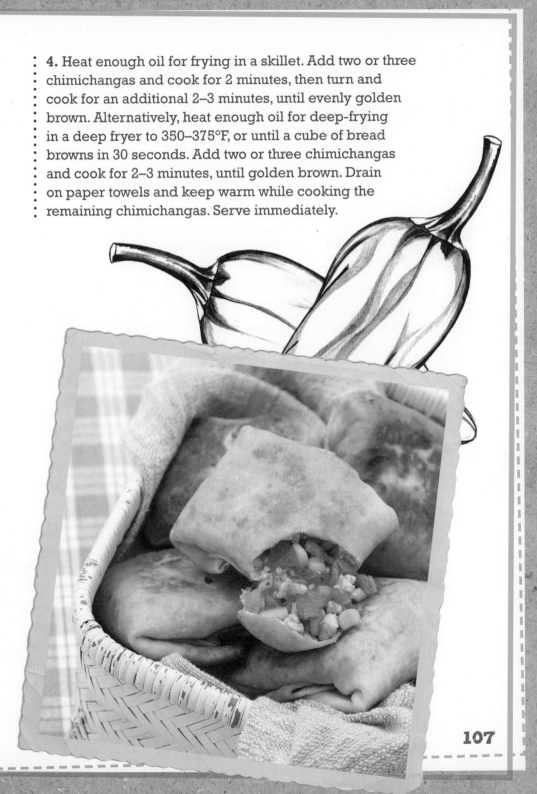

# TURKEY & CHORIZO PUFF PASTRIES

**MAKES: 8**          **PREP TIME: 30 MINS**          **COOK TIME: 30-35 MINS**

## INGREDIENTS

2 tablespoons vegetable oil, plus extra for greasing

1 onion, finely chopped

2 garlic cloves, finely chopped

8 ounces ground turkey

2 ounces chorizo sausage, finely chopped

2 teaspoons smoked paprika

1 yellow bell pepper, seeded and finely chopped

½ cup frozen peas

2 tablespoons fresh flat-leaf parsley, finely chopped

1 pound ready-to-bake rolled dough pie crust, thawed if frozen

1 medium egg, beaten

salt and pepper, to taste

**1.** Preheat the oven to 350°F. Heat the oil in a nonstick skillet, add the onion, and cook for 4–5 minutes, until softened. Add the garlic and cook for an additional 1 minute.

**2.** Add the ground turkey, chorizo, paprika, and yellow bell pepper and continue to cook for an additional 6–8 minutes, until the turkey is evenly browned. Stir in the peas and parsley, and season with salt and pepper.

**3.** Roll out the dough on a lightly floured work surface and use a saucer to cut out 8 circles. Spoon a small amount of the filling onto one half of each circle. Use a pastry brush to brush the edges of the pastry with a little beaten egg and fold the circles in half over the filling, crimping the edges to form a tight seal.

**4.** Lightly grease a baking pan with oil. Place the puff pastries on the prepared pan and brush each one with the remaining beaten egg. Bake in the preheated oven for 15–18 minutes, until golden. Serve immediately.

# BEEF & PINE NUT PUFF PASTRIES

**MAKES: 15**        **PREP TIME: 30–40 MINS    COOK TIME: 30–35 MINS**

## INGREDIENTS

1 tablespoon olive oil

1 small onion, chopped

2 garlic cloves, finely chopped

1 teaspoon ground coriander

1 teaspoon ground cumin

12 ounces ground beef

¼ cup chopped fresh mint

2 tablespoons pine nuts

2 Yukon gold or russet potatoes, peeled and cut into chunks

½ cup shredded American or cheddar cheese

1 stick butter, melted

10 sheets phyllo pastry

salt, to taste

tomato and basil salsa, to serve

**1.** Heat the oil in a large skillet. Add the onion and garlic and cook over low heat, stirring occasionally, for 5 minutes, until softened. Stir in the coriander and cumin and cook, stirring occasionally, for an additional 3 minutes. Add the beef, half the mint, and the pine nuts. Increase the heat to medium and cook, stirring and breaking up the meat with a wooden spoon, for 8–10 minutes, until evenly browned. Season with salt.

**2.** Meanwhile, cook the potatoes in a saucepan of salted boiling water for 15–20 minutes, until tender but not falling apart. Drain, transfer to a bowl and mash well, then stir in the cheese until melted. Stir in the beef mixture.

**3.** Preheat the oven to 400°F. Brush two baking sheets with melted butter. Brush one sheet of phyllo with melted butter, put a second sheet on top, and brush with more melted butter. Cut the double layer lengthwise into three strips. Put a heaping tablespoon of the filling near one end of a strip, then fold over the corner to form a triangle. Continue to fold over in triangles to make a neat package, then place on a prepared baking sheet. Make 14 more triangles in the same way. Brush with melted butter and bake in the preheated oven for 8–10 minutes, until golden brown. Serve the pastry triangles with a warm tomato and basil salsa.

# BEEF & MOZZARELLA RISOTTO BALLS

**SERVES: 4**

**PREP TIME: 30 MINS PLUS COOLING**

**COOK TIME: 1 HR**

## INGREDIENTS

1½ cups long-grain rice

4 tablespoons butter

2 tablespoons grated Parmesan cheese

1 tablespoon chopped fresh parsley

1 tablespoon olive oil

1 shallot, finely chopped

1 garlic clove, finely chopped

4 ounces ground beef

½ cup dry white wine

2 tablespoons tomato paste

4 ounces mozzarella cheese, cut into cubes

2 eggs

⅓ cup all-purpose flour

sunflower oil, for deep-frying

salt and pepper, to taste

**1.** Cook the rice in a large saucepan of salted boiling water for 15 minutes, until tender. Drain, rinse with boiling water, and return to the pan. Stir in half the butter, the Parmesan cheese, and parsley. Spread out on a baking sheet and let cool.

**2.** Meanwhile, melt the remaining butter with the olive oil in a saucepan. Add the shallot and garlic and cook over low heat, stirring occasionally, for 5 minutes, until softened. Add the beef, increase the heat to medium, and cook, stirring frequently and breaking it up with a wooden spoon, for 5–8 minutes, until evenly browned. Stir in the wine and cook for 5 minutes. Reduce the heat and stir in the tomato paste, then cover and simmer for 15 minutes. Season with salt and pepper.

**3.** When the rice is cold, shape into balls. Make a small hollow in each and put a spoonful of meat mixture and a cube of cheese inside, then reshape to enclose the filling. Lightly beat the eggs in a dish and spread out the flour in a separate dish. Dip the balls in the egg and then in the flour. Heat enough sunflower oil for deep-frying in a deep fryer to 350–375°F, or until a cube of bread browns in 30 seconds. Cook the balls, in batches, until golden brown, and serve immediately.

# BEEF CROQUETTES

SEVES: 6          PREP TIME: 30 MINS          COOK TIME: 35–45 MINS
PLUS CHILLING

## INGREDIENTS

9 Yukon gold or russet potatoes, peeled and cut into chunks

1 onion, finely chopped

1 pound ground beef

1 tablespoon snipped fresh chives

1 tablespoon chopped fresh parsley

2 teaspoon Worcestershire sauce or ketchup

3 eggs

3 tablespoons all-purpose flour

3½ cups fresh bread crumbs

sunflower oil, for pan-frying

salt and pepper, to taste

1. Cook the potatoes in a large saucepan of salted boiling water for 20–25 minutes, until tender but not falling apart. Drain well, tip into a bowl and mash the potatoes until smooth.

2. Add the onion, beef, chives, parsley, and Worcestershire sauce and season with salt and pepper. Mix well until thoroughly combined. Cover the bowl with plastic wrap and chill the mixture in the refrigerator for 30–45 minutes, until firm.

3. Dampen your hands and shape the mixture into 12 log-shaped croquettes. Lightly beat the eggs in a shallow dish, spread out the flour in a second shallow dish, and spread out the bread crumbs in a third shallow dish.

4. Pour oil into a large skillet to a depth of about ½ inch and heat. Meanwhile, coat the croquettes first in the flour, then in the beaten egg, and, finally, in the bread crumbs. Shake off any excess.

5. Add the croquettes to the skillet, in batches if necessary, and cook over medium heat, turning occasionally, for 8–10 minutes, until crisp, evenly browned, and cooked through. Remove from the skillet with a spatula and keep warm while you cook the remaining croquettes. Serve immediately.

# BEEF & MUSHROOM WONTONS

**MAKES: 12–15**          **PREP TIME: 30 MINS**          **COOK TIME: 15 MINS**

## INGREDIENTS

12–15 square wonton wrappers

peanut oil, for deep-frying

### SOY-GINGER DIPPING SAUCE

3 tablespoons soy sauce

2 teaspoon finely grated fresh ginger

### FILLING

4 ounces ground round or sirloin beef

1 scallion, green part included, finely chopped

2 white button mushrooms, finely chopped

1 small garlic clove, finely chopped

½ teaspoon finely chopped fresh ginger

½ teaspoon soy sauce

¼ teaspoon salt

¼ teaspoon freshly ground white pepper

⅛ teaspoon five-spice powder

½ teaspoon cornstarch

1 egg, beaten

1. To make the dipping sauce, combine the soy sauce and ginger in a small serving bowl. Set aside.

2. To make the filling, combine the ground beef, scallion, mushrooms, garlic, and ginger in a bowl. Mix the soy sauce, salt, pepper, five-spice powder, and cornstarch to a thin paste. Add the paste to the beef mixture, then stir in half the beaten egg. Stir with a fork until well mixed.

3. Separate the wonton squares and place on a pan, rotating them so that one corner is facing toward you. Cover with a clean damp dish towel to prevent them from cracking. Working with one square at a time, place a slightly rounded teaspoon of filling in the bottom corner ½ inch away from the point. Fold the point over the filling, then roll up two thirds of the wrapper, leaving a point at the top. Moisten the right- and left-hand corners with a dab of water. Fold one corner over the other and press lightly to seal. Continue until all the wontons are filled.

4. Heat enough oil for deep-frying in a large wok to 350–375°F, or until a cube of bread browns in 30 seconds. Deep-fry the wontons in batches for 4–5 minutes, until golden brown. Remove with tongs and drain on paper towels. Serve with the dipping sauce.

# FAIL-SAFE FRIENDS

Once you have chosen and created your tasty dish from the tempting selection of ground–meat recipes in this book, you might then be wondering what to serve with the dish to complete your meal. Here are a few quick and simple ideas for accompaniments that go well with some of the recipes to make your mealtimes even more enjoyable.

• Oven-baked or deep-fried homemade fries are the perfect accompaniment for hamburgers. Once cooked, season the hot fries lightly with salt and black pepper and serve alongside the burgers. Try serving with Bacon-wrapped Chicken Burgers (page 14) or Pork and Rosemary Burgers (page 32).

• Potato wedges (made with either standard or sweet potatoes) are a great alternative to fries. Serve plain or season them before baking with Cajun seasoning, Jamaican jerk seasoning, lemon, or garlic pepper or another seasoning mix of your choice. Alternatively, toss the hot baked wedges with some finely chopped fresh parsley or chives just before serving. Great served with Hamburgers (page 26) or Turkey Pot Pie (page 16).

• Serve soft, cooked cornmeal (either plain or flavored with chopped fresh herbs, such as thyme or rosemary, or dried crushed red pepper flakes and shredded cheddar cheese) or pan-fried or grilled herbed polenta slices, with tasty meatballs and sauce, such as Beef Meatballs with Sichuan Chili Sauce (page 58).

• Cook long-grain rice with flavorings such as cinnamon sticks and cracked green cardamom pods, to make delicious fragrant rice to serve with ground-meat dishes (remove the spices before serving the rice). Try serving with Chili Lamb (page 68) or Chili con Carne (page 52) instead of plain boiled rice.

• Add flavor to cooked couscous or bulgur wheat by adding chopped salad greens, such as watercress or arugula, scallions, and cucumber, and tossing with a light lemon, herb or chili dressing. Serve with kebabs/skewers or meatballs and sauce.

• Golden and crisp roasted mixed root vegetables (such as sweet potatoes, celeriac, carrots, and parsnips) create a tasty starchy side dish, ideal for serving with dishes such as Meatloaf (page 24).

• Sticky, glazed honey-roasted beets or caramelized roasted shallots go well with dishes such as Chicken-Stuffed Squash (page 12).

• Toss chunks of prepared vegetables (such as mixed bell peppers, zucchini, and red onions) in some oil, add some chopped garlic (and a little chopped fresh thyme too, if you desire), season with salt and pepper, and roast in a fairly hot oven until soft and lightly charred. Add some cherry tomatoes or plum tomato wedges toward the end of the roasting time. Perfect served with grilled burgers or kebabs/skewers.

• Minted peas and green beans, or green beans with hazelnut dressing go well with Lamb & Mashed Potato Pie (page 38).

• Sometimes a simple side dish is all you need. Stir-fried greens, wilted spinach with shallots, buttered leeks, a mixed leafy green salad, homemade crunchy coleslaw (with sunflower or pumpkin seeds added for extra crunch), or a mixed vegetable salad with a light and tasty dressing create quick and easy accompaniments for dishes such as Ground Beef Pizza (page 28), Meatball Risotto (page 36), or Turkey and Mushroom Cannelloni (page 78).

• Instead of plain mashed potatoes, create other tasty mashes by combining and cooking standard potatoes with celeriac, sweet potatoes, parsnips, or carrots. Season the hot mashed vegetables with black pepper and fresh herbs, such as snipped chives or chopped flat-leaf parsley. Great served with meatballs and sauce, or used as a topping for a casserole, or try serving with Turkey Stroganoff (page 82).

# CRISPY PORK DUMPLINGS

Store-bought wonton wrappers make these crispy dumplings a cinch to prepare. As well as a fantastic appetizer, you can also serve as a main dish, allowing around 15 dumplings per person.

**MAKES: 20**　　　　**PREP TIME: 15 MINS**　　　　**COOK TIME: 15 MINS**

## INGREDIENTS

3 scallions, coarsely chopped

1 garlic clove, coarsely chopped

1 small fresh red chile, seeded and coarsely chopped

8 ounces ground pork

20 wonton wrappers

peanut oil or vegetable oil, for deep-frying

salt, to taste

1. Put the scallions, garlic, chile, and pork in a food processor and season with salt. Process to a smooth paste.

2. Remove the wonton wrappers from the package, but keep them in a pile and cover with a clean, damp dish towel to prevent them from drying out. Lay one wrapper on a work surface in front of you in a diamond shape and brush the edges with water. Put a small amount of filling near one edge and fold the wrapper over the filling. Press the edges together to seal the package and shape into a semicircle. Repeat with the remaining wrappers and filling.

3. Heat enough oil for deep-frying in a large wok to 350–375°F, or until a cube of bread browns in 30 seconds. Add the dumplings, in batches, and cook for 45 seconds–1 minute, until crisp and golden brown all over and the pork filling is cooked through. Remove with a slotted spoon, drain on paper towels, and keep warm while you cook the remaining dumplings. Serve immediately.

1

2

3

121

# SPRING ROLLS

With a tasty pork and shrimp filling, these crisp golden rolls are an irresistible appetizer.

**MAKES: 20**

**PREP TIME: 15 MINS PLUS COOLING**

**COOK TIME: 15 MINS**

## INGREDIENTS

6 dried Chinese mushrooms, soaked in warm water for 20 minutes

1 tablespoon vegetable oil or peanut oil, plus extra for deep-frying

8 ounces ground pork

1 teaspoon dark soy sauce

¾ cup rinsed canned bamboo shoots, julienned

pinch of salt

4 ounces raw shrimp, peeled, deveined, and chopped

2 cups coarsely chopped bean sprouts

1 tablespoon finely chopped scallions

20 spring roll wrappers

1 egg white, lightly beaten

**1.** Squeeze out any excess water from the mushrooms and finely slice, discarding any tough stems.

**2.** Heat a wok over high heat, then add the oil. Add the pork and stir-fry until the pork is cooked through and no longer pink.

**3.** Add the dark soy sauce, bamboo shoots, mushrooms, and a little salt. Stir over high heat for 3 minutes.

**4.** Add the shrimp and cook for 2 minutes, until they turn pink and start to curl. Add the bean sprouts and cook for an additional minute. Remove from the heat and stir in the scallions. Let cool.

**5.** Place a tablespoon of the mixture toward the bottom of a wrapper. Roll once to secure the filling, then fold in the sides to create a 4-inch piece and continue to roll up. Seal with egg white.

**6.** Heat enough oil for deep-frying in a large wok to 350–375°F, or until a cube of bread browns in 30 seconds. Cook the rolls for about 5 minutes, until golden brown and crispy.

# PORK & CABBAGE DUMPLINGS

**MAKES: 24**          **PREP TIME: 30–35 MINS    COOK TIME: 20–25 MINS**

## INGREDIENTS

24 wonton wrappers

2 tablespoons water,
for brushing

oil, for pan-frying

2 tablespoons rice vinegar

2 tablespoons soy sauce

## FILLING

1½ cups finely shredded
napa cabbage

2 scallions, finely chopped

4 ounces pork mince

½-inch piece fresh ginger,
finely grated

2 garlic cloves, crushed

1 tablespoon soy sauce

2 teaspoon mirin

pinch of white pepper

salt, to taste

**1.** To make the filling, mix all the ingredients together in a bowl.

**2.** Lay a wonton wrapper in the palm of your hand and place a heaping teaspoon of the filling in the center. Brush a little water around the edges of the wonton wrapper.

**3.** Fold the wrapper sides up to meet in a ridge along the center and press the edges together. Brush the curved edges of the wrapper with a little more water and make a series of little folds along the edges.

**4.** Repeat with the remaining wonton wrappers and filling. Heat a little oil in a deep lidded skillet and add as many packages as will fill the bottom of the skillet with just a little space in between.

**5.** Cook for 2 minutes, or until browned. Add water to a depth of ⅛ inch, cover the skillet, and simmer over low heat for 6 minutes, or until the wrappers are translucent and cooked. Remove and keep warm while you cook the remaining dumplings.

**6.** Put the vinegar in a small dipping dish, stir in the soy, and add a splash of water.

**7.** Transfer the dumplings to a serving dish and serve with the sauce for dipping.

# LAMB SKEWERS WITH MASHED CHICKPEAS

**SERVES: 4**

**PREP TIME: 25 MINS PLUS CHILLING**

**COOK TIME: 25-30 MINS**

## INGREDIENTS

8 ounces lean ground lamb
1 onion, finely chopped
1 tablespoon chopped fresh cilantro
1 tablespoon chopped fresh parsley
½ teaspoon ground coriander
¼ teaspoon chili powder
oil, for brushing
salt and pepper, to taste

## MASHED CHICKPEAS

1 tablespoon olive oil
2 garlic cloves, chopped
1 (15-ounce) can chickpeas, drained and rinsed
¼ cup milk
2 tablespoons chopped fresh cilantro
salt and pepper, to taste
cilantro sprigs, to garnish

**1.** Put the lamb, onion, herbs, and spices in a food processor and season with salt and pepper. Process until thoroughly combined.

**2.** Divide the mixture into 12 portions, and, using wet hands, shape each portion into a log shape around a wooden skewer (soaked in water first to prevent them from burning). Cover and chill the skewers in the refrigerator for 30 minutes.

**3.** To cook, preheat a ridged grill pan over medium heat and brush with a little oil. Cook the skewers in two batches, turning occasionally, for 10 minutes, or until browned on all sides and cooked through.

**4.** To make the mashed chickpeas, heat the oil in a saucepan and gently sauté the garlic for 2 minutes. Add the chickpeas and milk and heat through for a few minutes. Transfer to a food processor or blender and process until smooth. Season with salt and pepper, then stir in the fresh cilantro. Garnish with cilantro sprigs and serve with the skewers.

# INDEX